The Bee Safe Crew
Copyright © 2022 by Shaundria Nunley
ISBN Print Book: 978-1-0878-7631-3
All rights reserved.

No part of this book may be used or reproduced by any means, graphic, electronic, or mechanical, including photocopying, recording, taping, or by information storage retrieval system without the publisher's written permission except in the case of brief quotation embodied in critical articles and reviews.

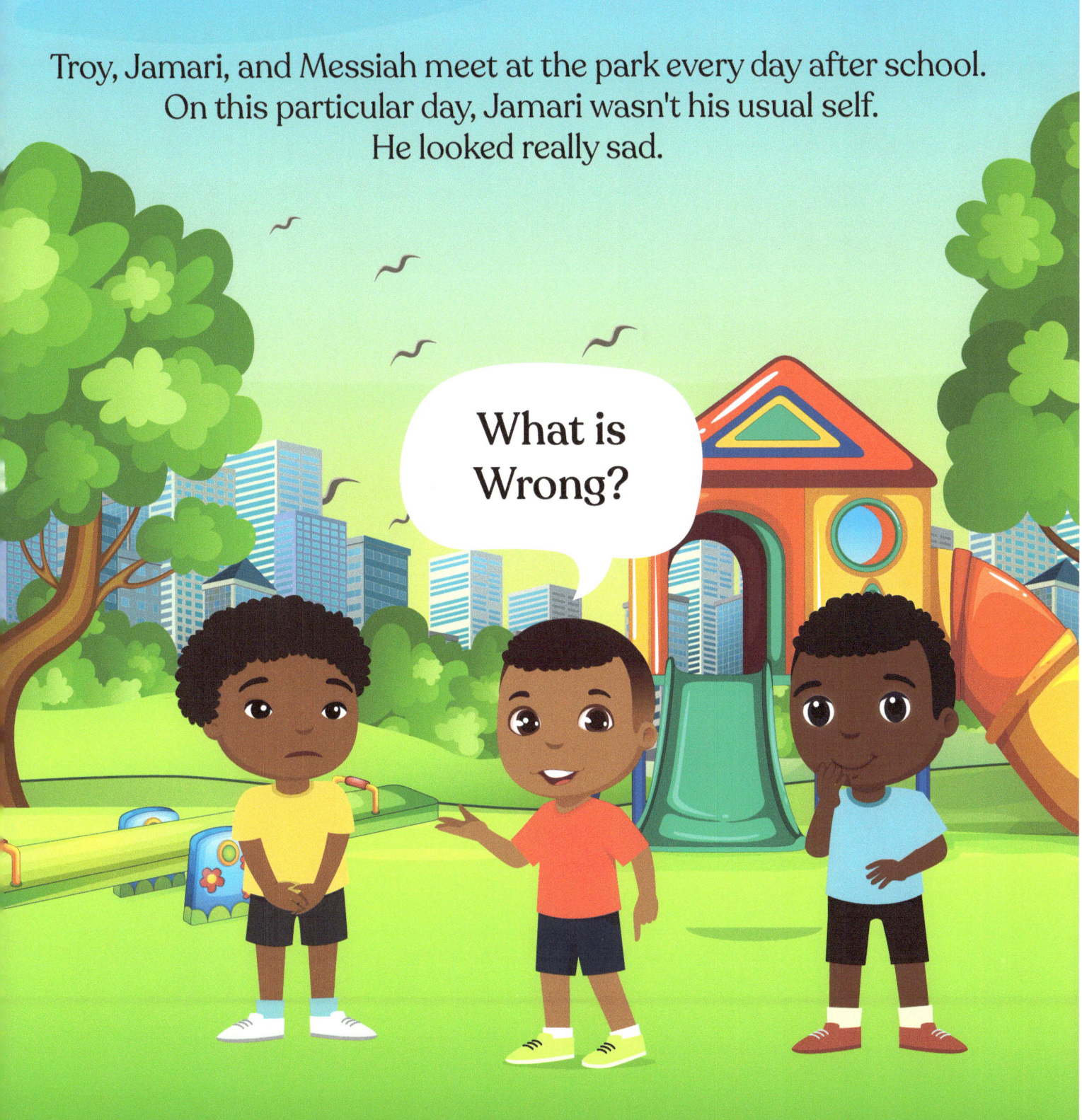

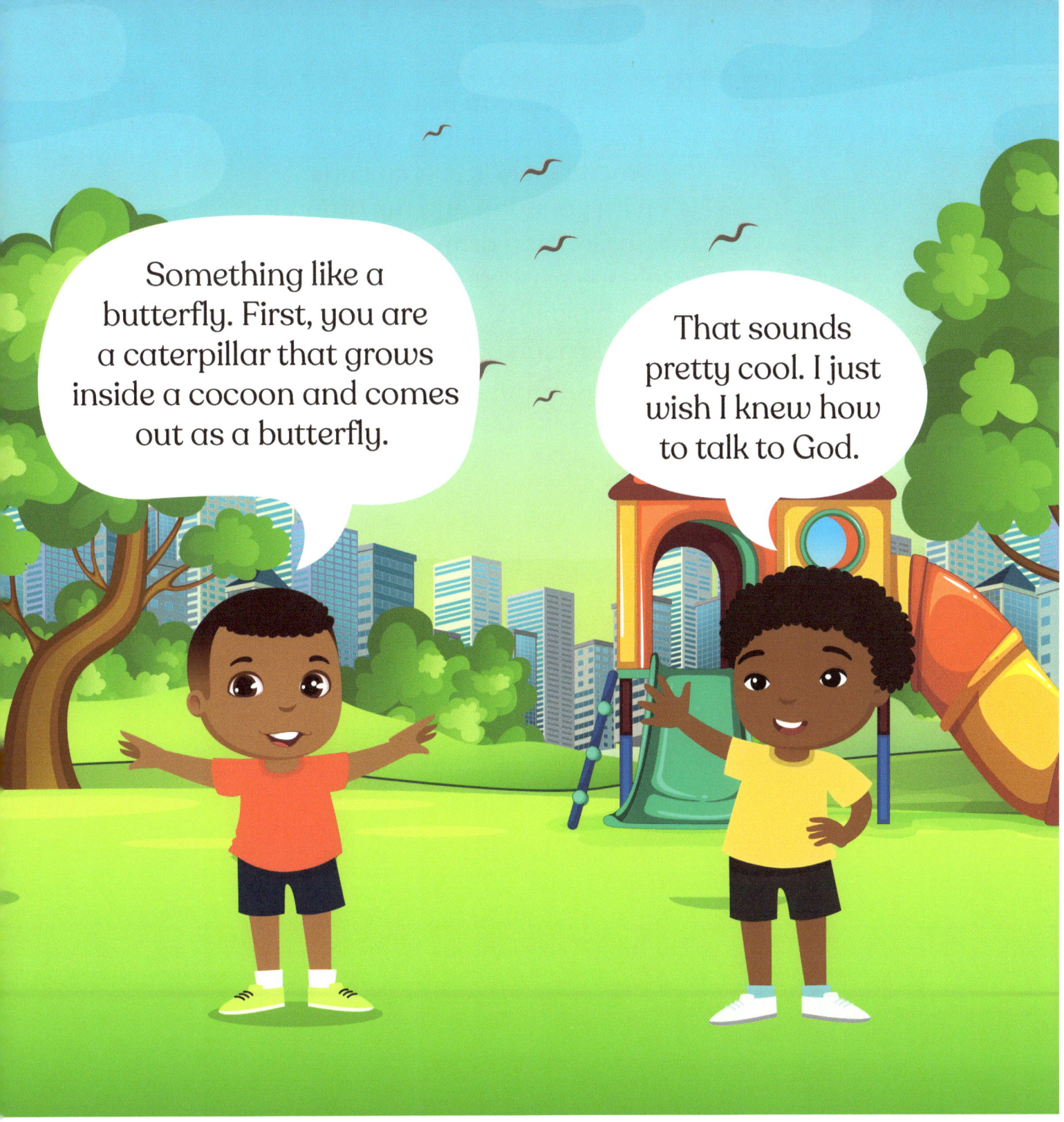

Thank you, Father God, for waking me up. Protect me from any evil. Surround me with the armor of God. Direct my path, for I shall serve you all the days of my life. Bless me with wisdom, strength, and power to do Your will here on the earth as it is in heaven. In Jesus' Name, Amen!

Our Father which art in heaven, Hallowed be thy name. Thy kingdom come, Thy will be done in earth, as it is in heaven. Give us this day our daily bread. And forgive us our debts, as we forgive our debtors. And lead us not into temptation, but deliver us from evil: For thine is the kingdom, and the power, and the glory, for ever. Amen.

Shaundria Nunley

Shaundria is a strong woman of God who has overcome many obstacles that began with being sexually violated by her father at a very early age. She has fought through many trials and tribulations in her life.

Shaundria is an advocate for children and started a non-profit foundation called BeeSafe Kids after the untimely murder of her son in 2012. This organization brings awareness to rape, bullying, sex trafficking, physical abuse, and mental abuse.

Shaundria is a member of Fountain of Praise Church and has truly grown in God under the leadership of Pastors Remus and Mia Wright. She has four children and two grandchildren.

Contact the Author:

Email: s.nunley46@gmail.com
Facebook: Shaundria Nunley

www.ingramcontent.com/pod-product-compliance
Lightning Source LLC
Chambersburg PA
CBHW041439010526
44118CB00002B/131